Houses

by Maria Johnson
illustrated by Doug Roy

Core Decodable 110

Mc Graw Hill Education

Bothell, WA • Chicago, IL • Columbus, OH • New York, NY

MHEonline.com

Send all inquiries to:
McGraw-Hill Education
8787 Orion Place
Columbus, OH 43240

ISBN: 978-0-02-145838-7
MHID: 0-02-145838-3

Printed in Canada.

9 10 11 12 KOD 24

Sunshine filled the yard. Josh rested on his shady porch. It was hot for the third week in May.

At the next house, Ruth checked her mail. "My nephew sent a postcard," she called. "He is in his house on the beach."

"His house is on the beach!" Josh thought. "I wish I had a house on the beach."

But he did not say that.

In early June, Josh painted a bench.

"My nephew wrote me," Ruth said. "He is in his house at the ranch."

"Wow," thought Josh. "Ruth's nephew has two houses! How did he pay for both?"

But he did not say that.

In late June, Josh cleaned his car.

"I heard from my nephew," Ruth said. "He is in his house at the river."

Now Josh thought, "Ruth's nephew must be rich. He has three houses."

But Josh did not say that.

It was later in the summer. Josh was making lunch for a bunch of pals. He heard a phone ring in Ruth's house.

Later, Ruth said, "I got a call from my nephew. He is in his house in the woods. He is searching for birds."

Josh was shocked. "Four houses!" he thought. "How can Ruth's nephew own four houses?"

But Josh did not say that.

In August, Josh brushed his dog's fur.

"My nephew sent a photo," said Ruth. "He is in his house in the far north."

"That is his fifth house!" thought Josh. "Ruth's nephew must be very, very rich."

But Josh still did not say that.

In September, Josh's phone rang. "Josh, this is Ruth," said a voice. "I am calling from my nephew's house in the street."

Josh looked out the window.

"I see the truth," he thought. "Ruth's nephew has just one house. It has wheels!"

Core Decodable 110

Houses

Previously Introduced High-Frequency Words

a	blue	for	him	make	said	too	with
about	boy	four	his	me	saw	two	would
after	brown	from	how	my	see	up	yellow
all	but	get	I	no	she	very	yes
am	by	girl	if	now	six	walk	you
an	call	go	in	of	sleep	want	your
and	came	going	into	old	some	was	
any	can	good	is	on	take	water	
are	come	got	it	one	that	way	
around	could	green	its	or	the	we	
as	day	had	jump	out	their	well	
ask	did	has	just	over	them	went	
at	do	have	know	pretty	then	were	
away	don't	he	like	put	there	what	
be	down	help	little	red	they	when	
before	every	her	long	ride	this	where	
big	five	here	look	right	to	will	

Sound/Spelling Correspondences in Core Decodables

1. Pre-decodable
2. Pre-decodable
3. Pre-decodable
4. Pre-decodable
5. Pre-decodable
6. /s/ spelled *s*, /m/ spelled *m*, /a/ spelled *a*
7. /t/ spelled *t*, *tt*
8. Review
9. /d/ spelled *d*
10. /n/ spelled *n*
11. /i/ spelled *i*
12. /h/ spelled *h_*
13. Review
14. /p/ spelled *p*
15. /l/ spelled *l*, *ll*
16. /o/ spelled *o*
17. /b/ spelled *b*
18. Review
19. /k/ spelled *c*
20. special spelling *al*, *all*
21. /k/ spelled *k*, *■ck*
22. /r/ spelled *r*
23. Review
24. /f/ spelled *f*, *ff*
25. /s/ spelled *ss*
26. /g/ spelled *g*
27. /j/ spelled *j*
28. Review
29. /j/ spelled *■dge*
30. /u/ spelled *u*
31. /z/ spelled *z*, *zz*
32. /z/ spelled *_s*
33. Review
34. /ks/ spelled *■x*
35. /e/ spelled *e*
36. *-ed* ending: /ed/, /d/
37. *-ed* ending: /t/
38. Review
39. /e/ spelled *_ea_*
40. /sh/ spelled *sh*
41. /th/ spelled *th*
42. /ch/ spelled *ch*, *■tch*
43. Review
44. /or/ spelled *or*, *ore*
45. /ar/ spelled *ar*
46. /w/ spelled *w_*
47. /w/ spelled *wh_*
48. Review
49. /er/ spelled *er*, *ir*
50. /er/ spelled *ur*
51. /er/ spelled *ear*
52. /ng/ spelled *■ng*
53. Review
54. Schwa
55. *-le*, *-el*, *-il*, *-al*
56. /nk/ spelled *■nk*
57. /kw/ spelled *qu_*
58. Review
59. /y/ spelled *y_*
60. /v/ spelled *v*
61. /ā/ spelled *a*, *a_e*
62. Review
63. /ī/ spelled *i*, *i_e*
64. /s/ spelled *ce*, *ci_*
65. /j/ spelled *ge*, *gi_*
66. Review
67. /ō/ spelled *o*, *o_e*
68. /ū/ spelled *u*, *u_e*
69. Review
70. /ē/ spelled *e*, *e_e*
71. /ē/ spelled *ee*, *ea*
72. Review /ē/
73. /ē/ spelled *_y*, *_ie_*
74. /ē/ spelled *_ey*
75. Review
76. /s/ spelled *cy*
77. /ā/ spelled *ai_*, *_ay*
78. Review
79. /ī/ spelled *igh*
80. /ī/ spelled *_y*, *_ie*
81. Review /ī/
82. /ō/ spelled *oa_*, *_ow*
83. /ū/ spelled *_ew*, *_ue*
84. Review
85. /m/ spelled *_mb*
86. /n/ spelled *kn_*, *gn*
87. /r/ spelled *wr_*
88. /f/ spelled *ph*
89. Review
90. /o͞o/ spelled *oo*
91. /o͞o/ spelled *u*, *_ue*
92. Review
93. /o͞o/ spelled *_ew*, *u_e*
94. /oo/ spelled *oo*
95. Review
96. /ow/ spelled *ow*
97. /ow/ spelled *ou_*
98. /aw/ spelled *au_*, *aw*
99. Review
100. /aw/ spelled *ough*
101. /oi/ spelled *oi*, *_oy*
102. Review
103. Prefixes *un-*, *dis-*
104. Prefixes *im-*, *in-*, *re-*
105. Review /ā/ and /a/
106. Review /ī/ and /i/
107. Review /ō/ and /o/
108. Review /ū/ and /u/
109. Review /ē/ and /e/
110. Review consonant digraphs

SRA Open Court Reading

Decodables

Grade 1
Core Decodable 110
Houses

MHEonline.com

978-0-02-145838-7
MHID 0-02-145838-3

EAN
9 780021 458387 99701

Mc Graw Hill Education